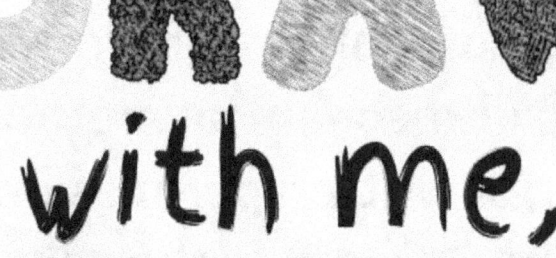

DRAW
with me,
MOM

A Mother-Child Daily Drawing Diary

OCTOBER

How to Use This Book

Welcome to "Draw with me". We're so excited to have you embark on this artistic journey with us. Here's a simple guide to make the most out of your drawing adventures:

1. **Pick a Prompt**:
Begin by flipping through the pages and selecting a drawing prompt that sparks interest. There's no need to go in order—follow where your creativity leads!

2. **Child's Play First**:
Each prompt has a section for the child and one for the parent. We recommend letting the child dive in first. Use their imagination, doodle, and lay the groundwork.

3. **Dad Joins In**:
Once the child has done their part, it's your turn to add your artistic touch. Remember, there's no right or wrong! It's all about enjoying the process and bonding.

4. **Discuss & Laugh**:
After both of you have completed your drawings, talk about them! Share what you loved, what made you giggle, and what surprised you.

5. **Date Your Art**:
At the bottom of each page, jot down the date. As you fill up the book, you'll love looking back and seeing how both of your skills and styles evolve.

6. **Share with Loved Ones**:
Proud of a particular page? Show it off! Grandparents, siblings, or friends would love to see your combined masterpieces.

Remember, this book is not just about drawing—it's about the cherished memories you create together. So, grab your crayons, colored pencils, or whatever you love to draw with, and let the fun begin!

Happy Drawing!

--

Child

Draw the spookiest haunted mansion on top of a hill.

Sketch the friendly ghost that lives inside of the mansion.

Mom

Child

Draw a witch flying over a full moon.

Design her unique, magical broomstick.

Mom

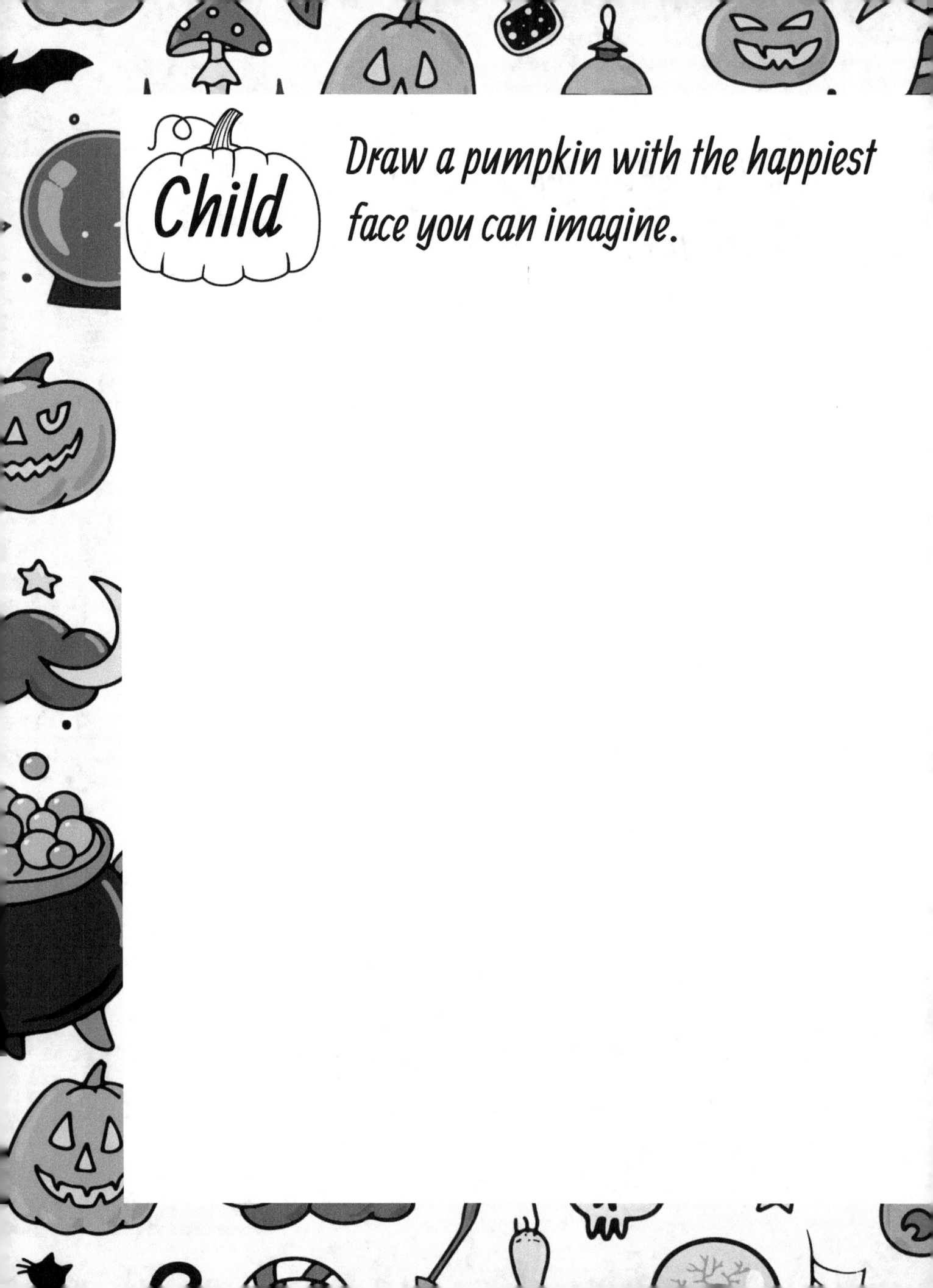

Child

Draw a pumpkin with the happiest face you can imagine.

Sketch a pumpkin with the most mischievous grin.

Mom

Child

Draw a forest where trees have faces.

Add the woodland creatures who throw a secret Halloween party there.

Mom

Child

Draw your ideal Halloween candy bucket filled to the top.

Illustrate the trail you'd take around your neighborhood to collect them. **Mom**

Child

Draw a vampire costume.

Draw a funny witch costume. **Mom**

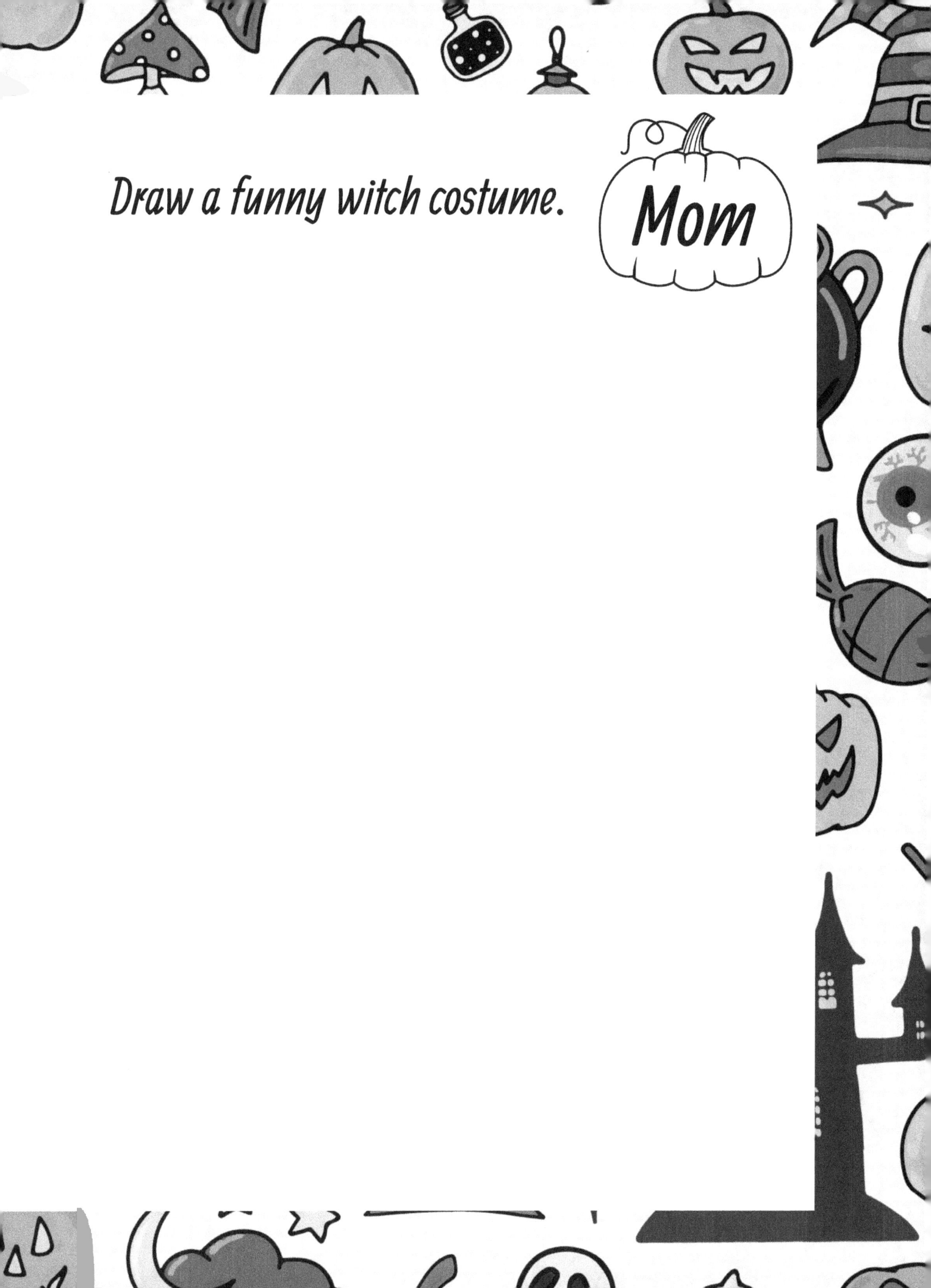

Child

Draw a mummy

llustrate what the mummy's pet would look like

Mom

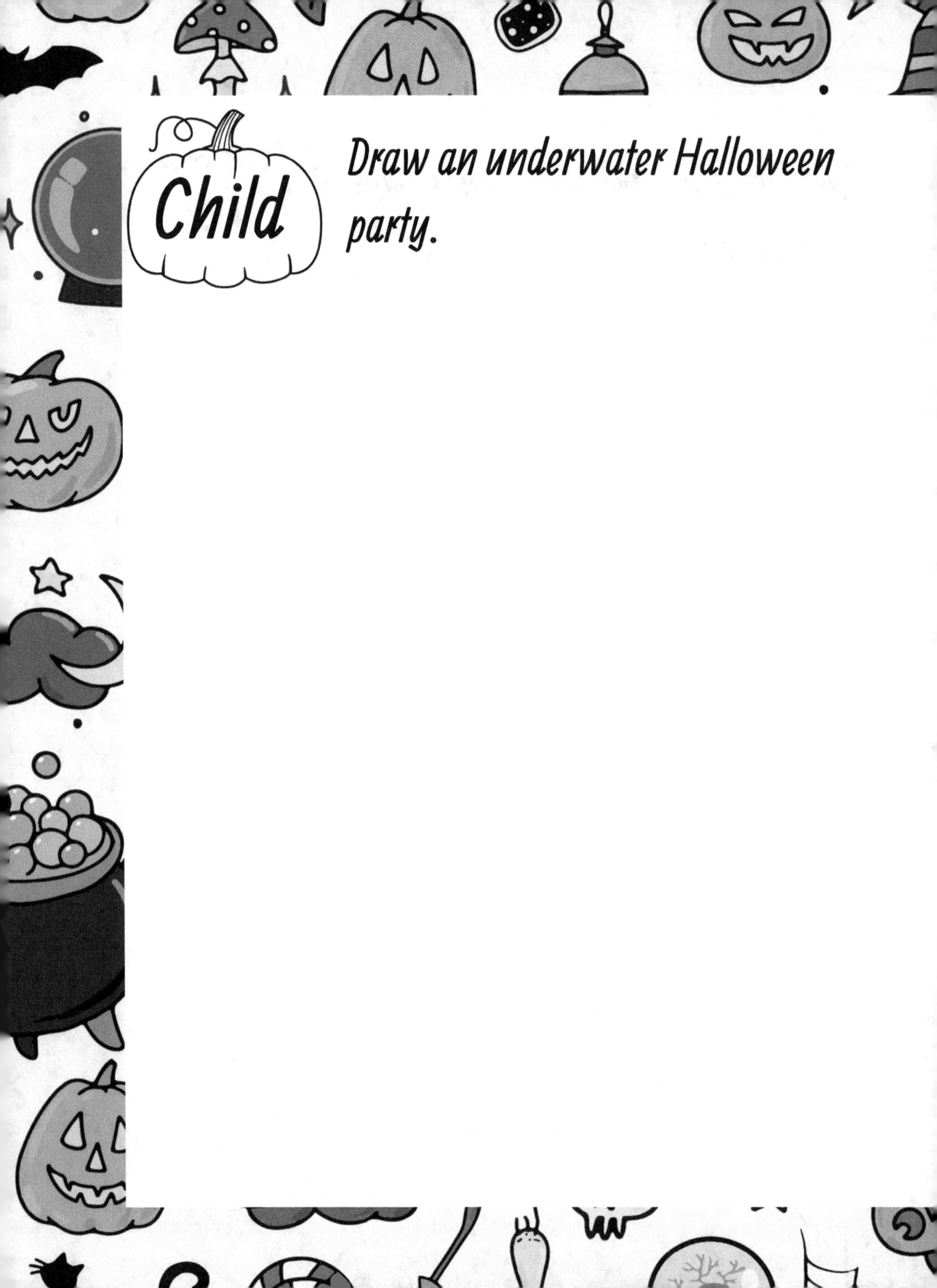

Child

Draw an underwater Halloween party.

Draw a mermaid dressed up for the occasion.

Mom

Child Draw a witch cooking up a magic potion.

Draw a magical creature who would visit the witch's shop.

Mom

Child

Sketch a skeleton showing its best dance move.

Draw the instrument that a second skeleton is playing to provide the tune. **Mom**

Child

Draw a fairy with bat wings.

Draw a bat with spiderweb wings. **Mom**

Child Draw a monster making a sandwich.

Draw the surprising ingredients the monster is using.

Mom

Child

Draw a witch's spellbook.

Draw a creature the witch conjures.

Mom

Child

Draw a ghost at a party.

Draw the balloon the ghost is holding, shaped like a famous monster.

Mom

Child

Draw an alien dressed as a human.

Draw the Earth pet it adopts.

Mom

Child

Draw a crown for the Pumpkin King.

Draw a tiara for the Witch Queen. **Mom**

Child

Draw spooky pasteries and bread that come to life at night.

Draw the baker ghost that makes them.

Mom

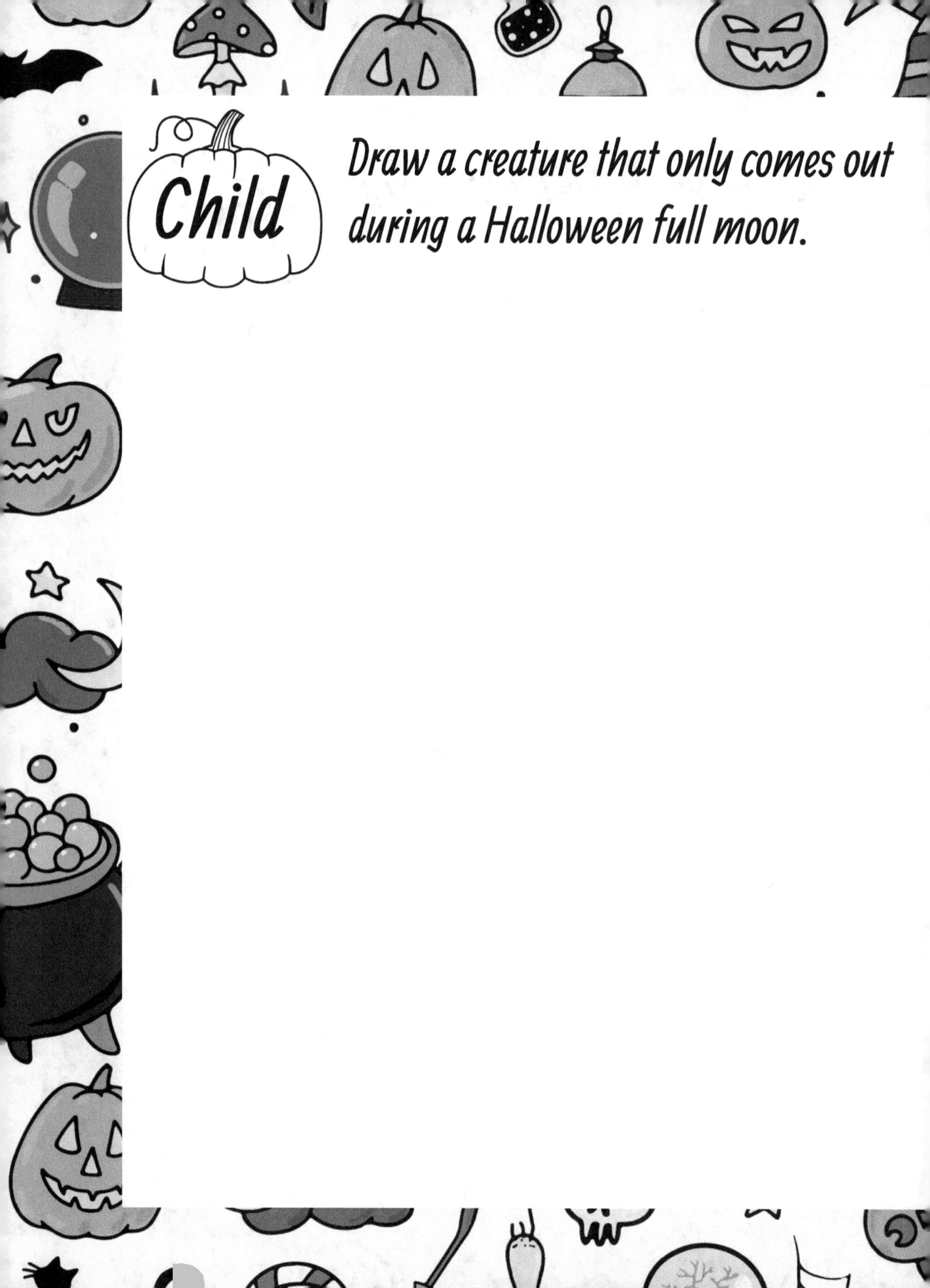

Child

Draw a creature that only comes out during a Halloween full moon.

Draw a creature that only comes out every 100 years.

Mom

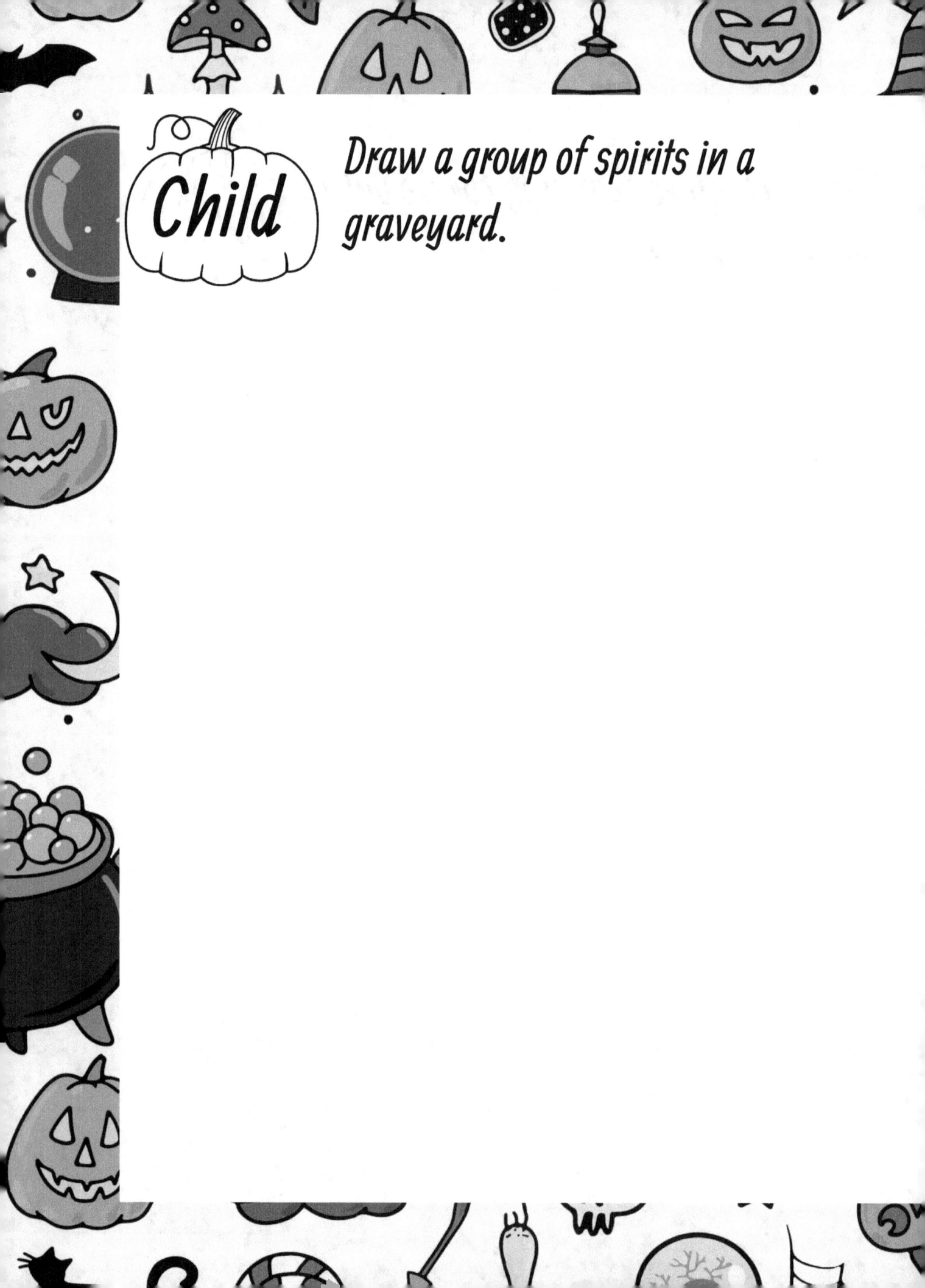

Child Draw a group of spirits in a graveyard.

Draw the spectral animal that joins them.

Child Draw a path lined with jack-o-lanterns leading to a mysterious place.

Draw what lies at the end of the path.

Mom

Child

Draw a witch's cat wearing its own tiny costume.

Illustrate the special magical power this cat possesses.

Mom

Child

Sketch a raven delivering a special Halloween message.

Draw the magical being who sent it. Mom

Child

Illustrate a ghostly train that only appears on Halloween.

Draw the passengers of this train. 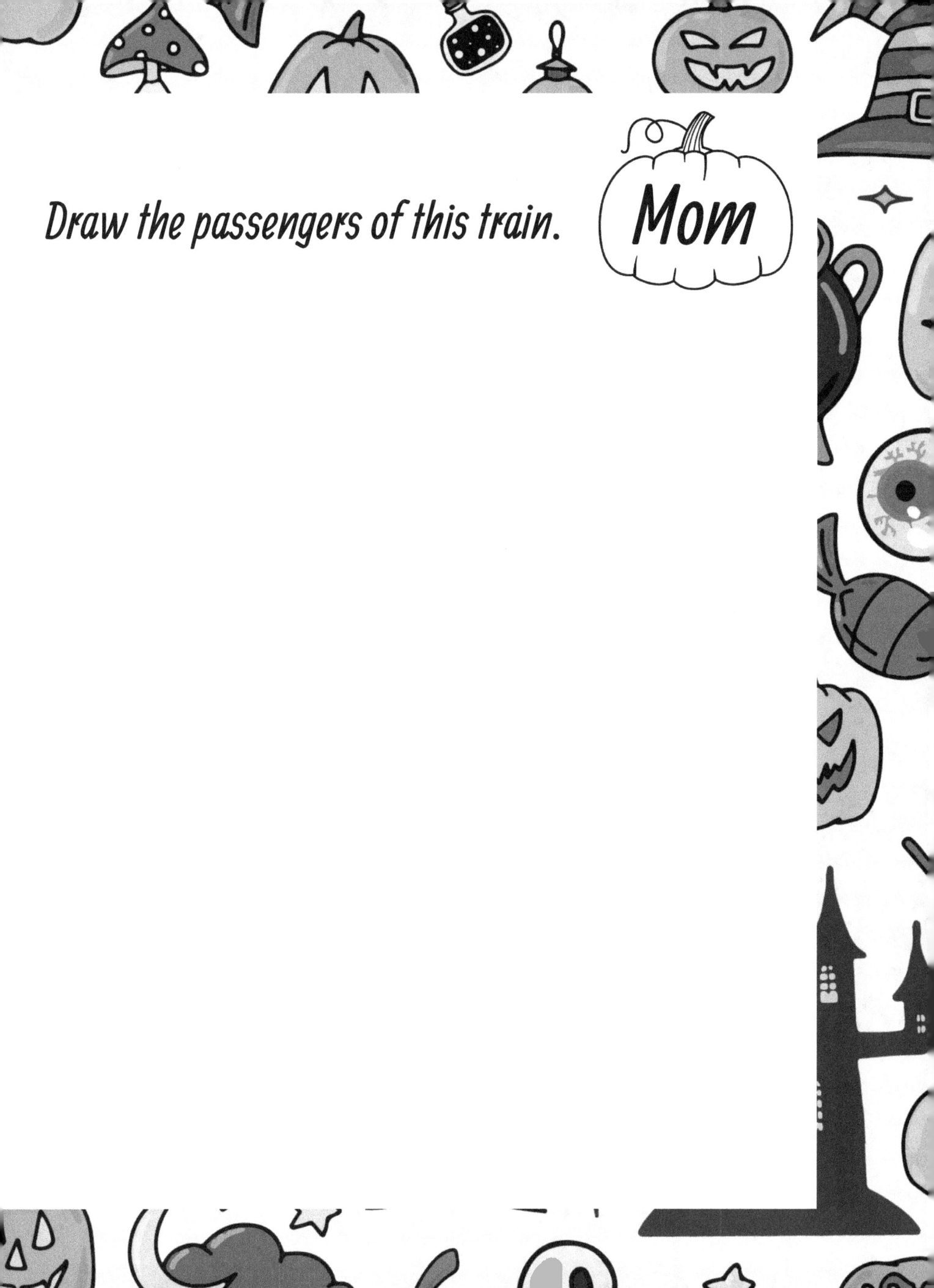 **Mom**

Child

Draw a castle made entirely of spiderwebs.

Draw the spiders that guard it.

Mom

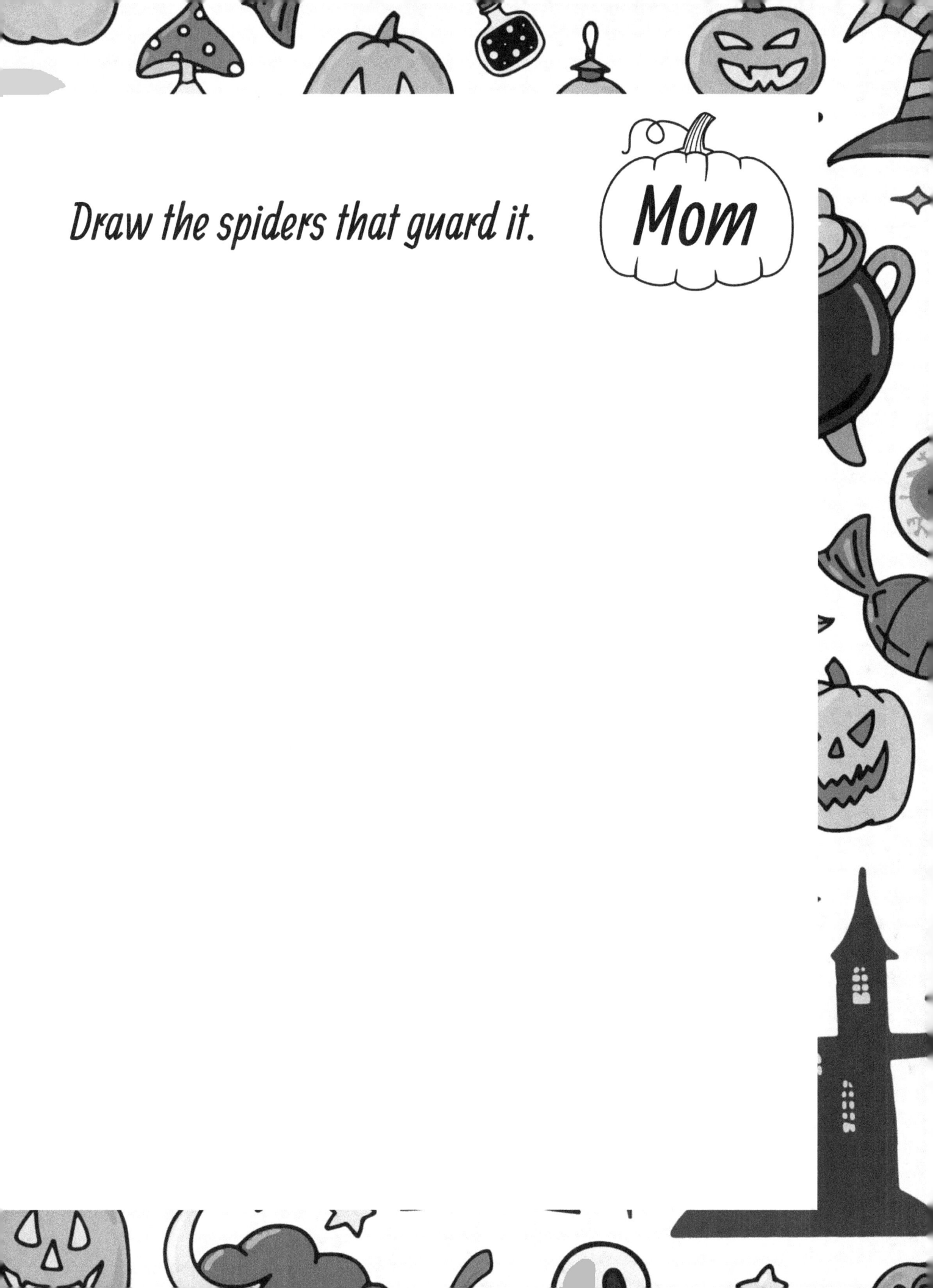

Child Draw Frankenstein at a Halloween Party.

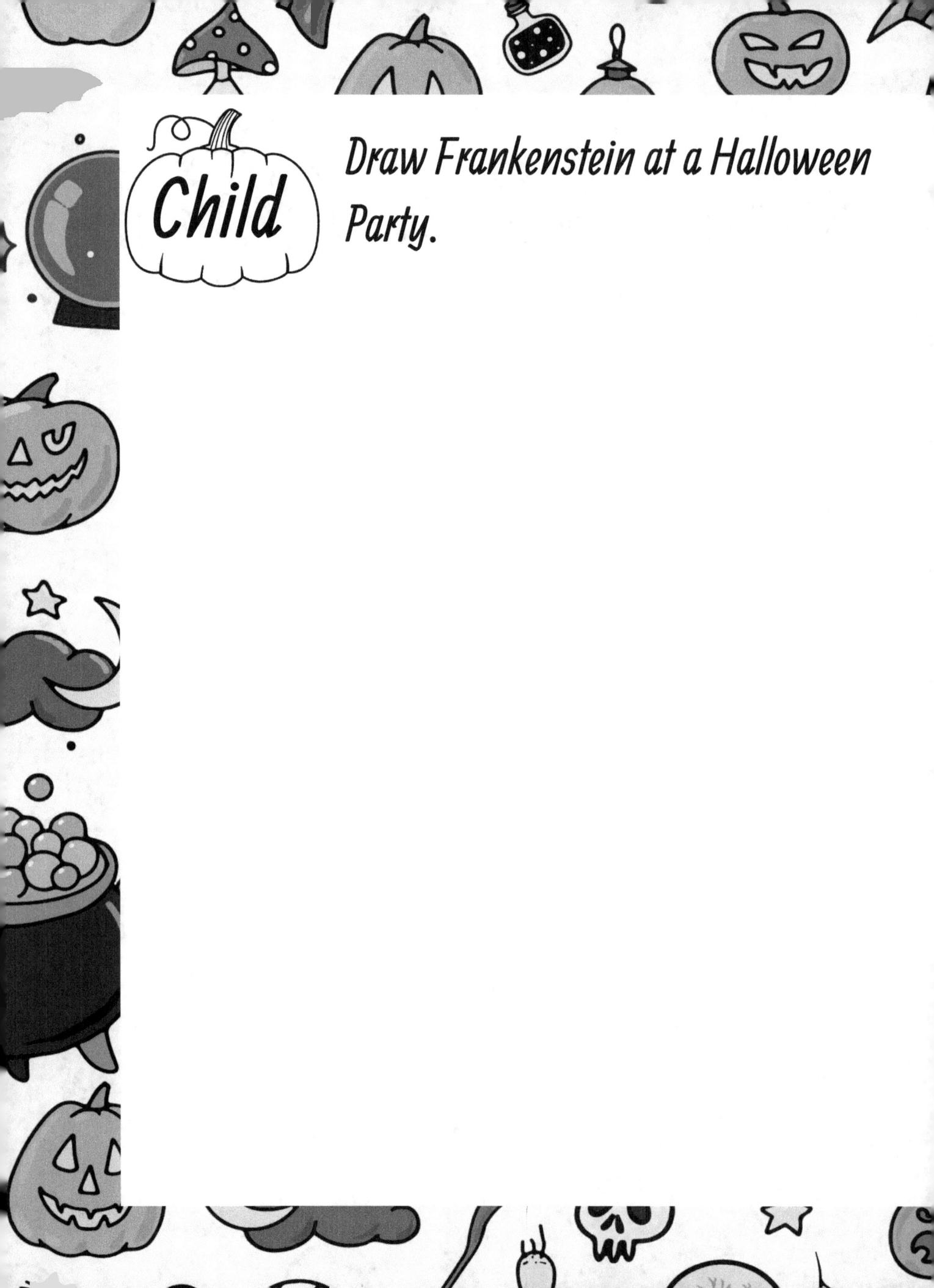

Draw the mask he is wearing. **Mom**

Let's mix it up a little with some
TIC TAC TOE!

In this next section you will choose what the other draws. You can also ask another family member to choose for extra fun!!

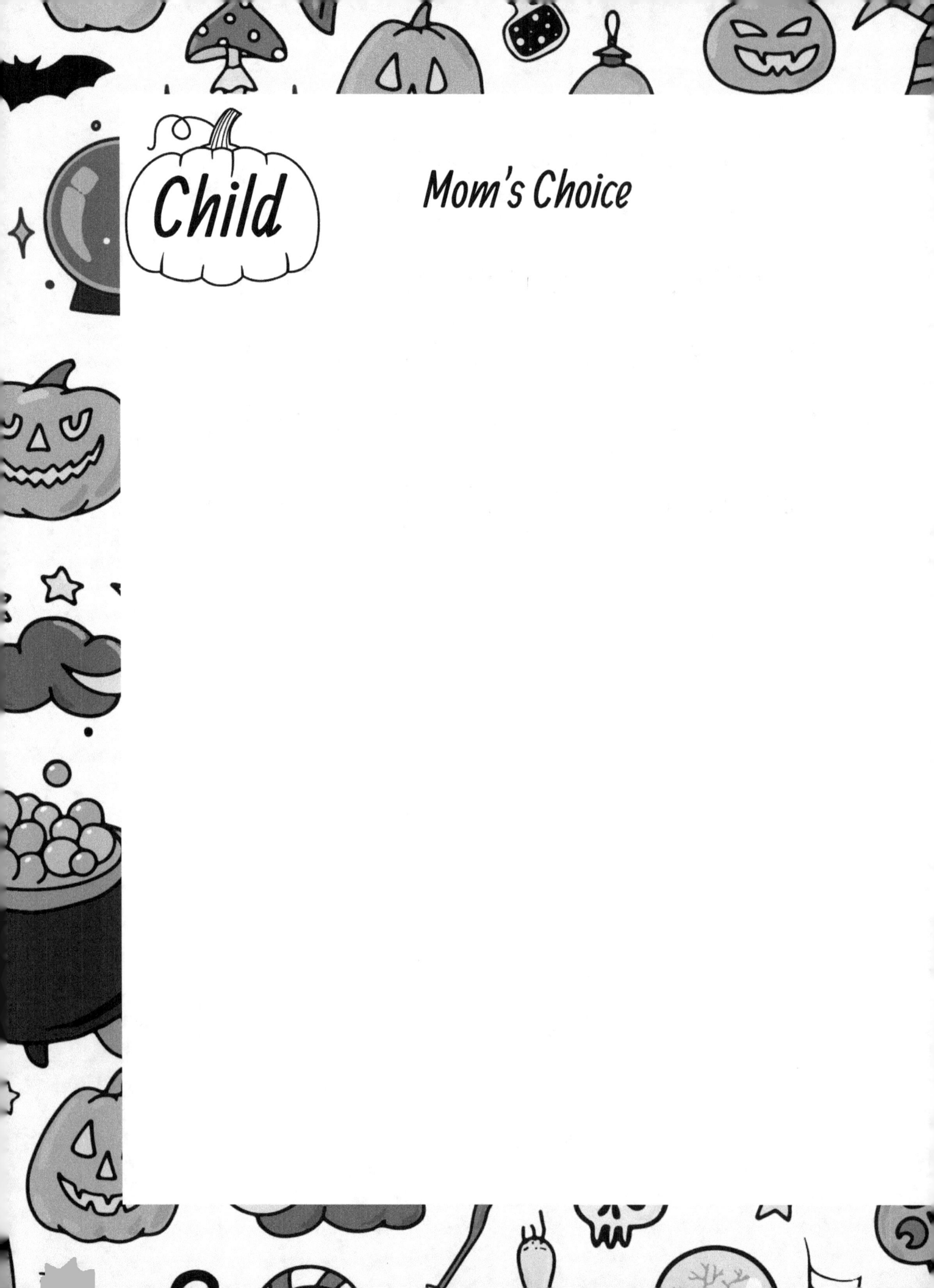

Child

Mom's Choice

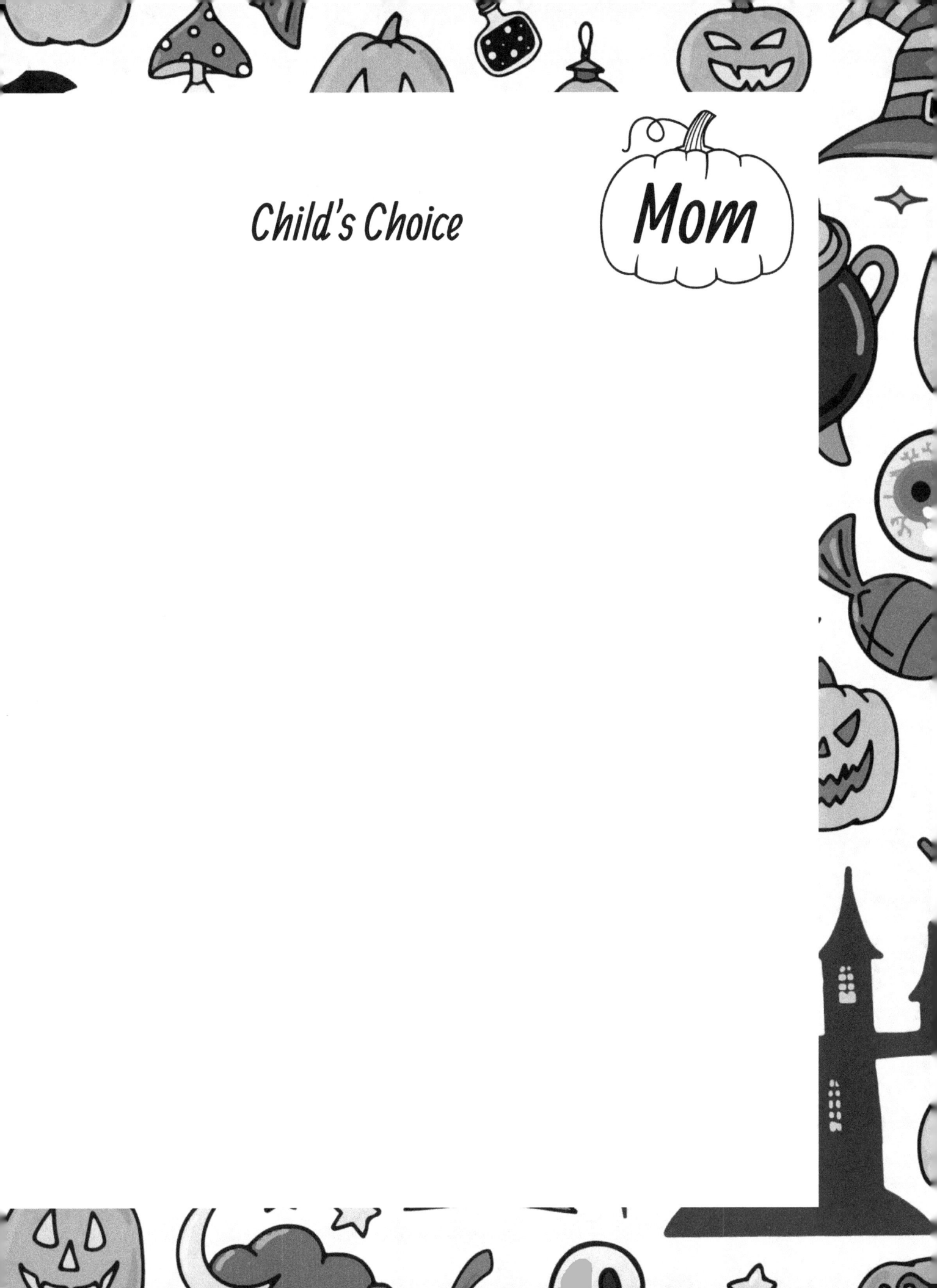

Child's Choice

Mom

Child

Mom's Choice

Child's Choice

Mom

Child

Mom's Choice

Child's Choice

Mom

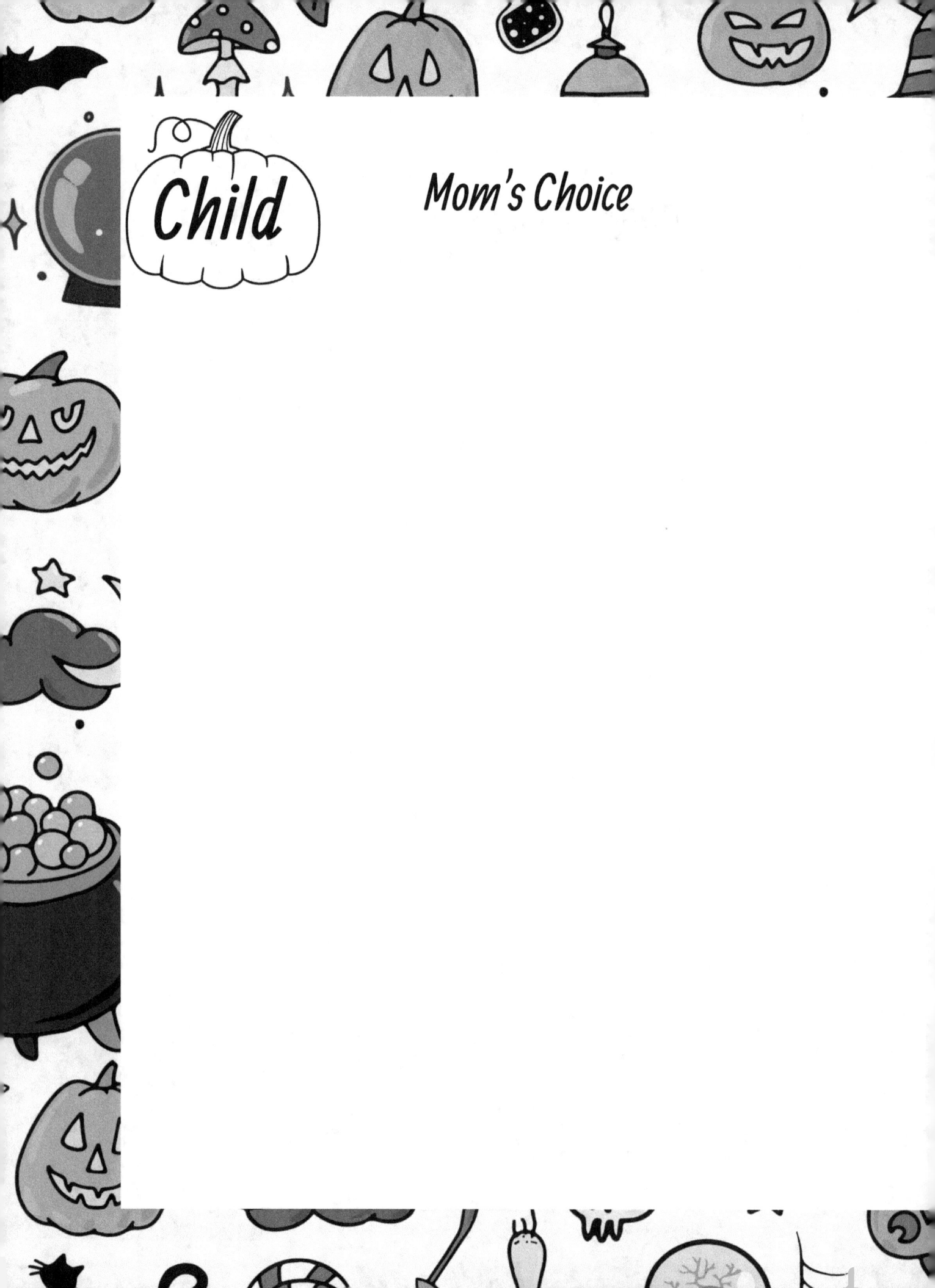

Child

Mom's Choice

Child's Choice

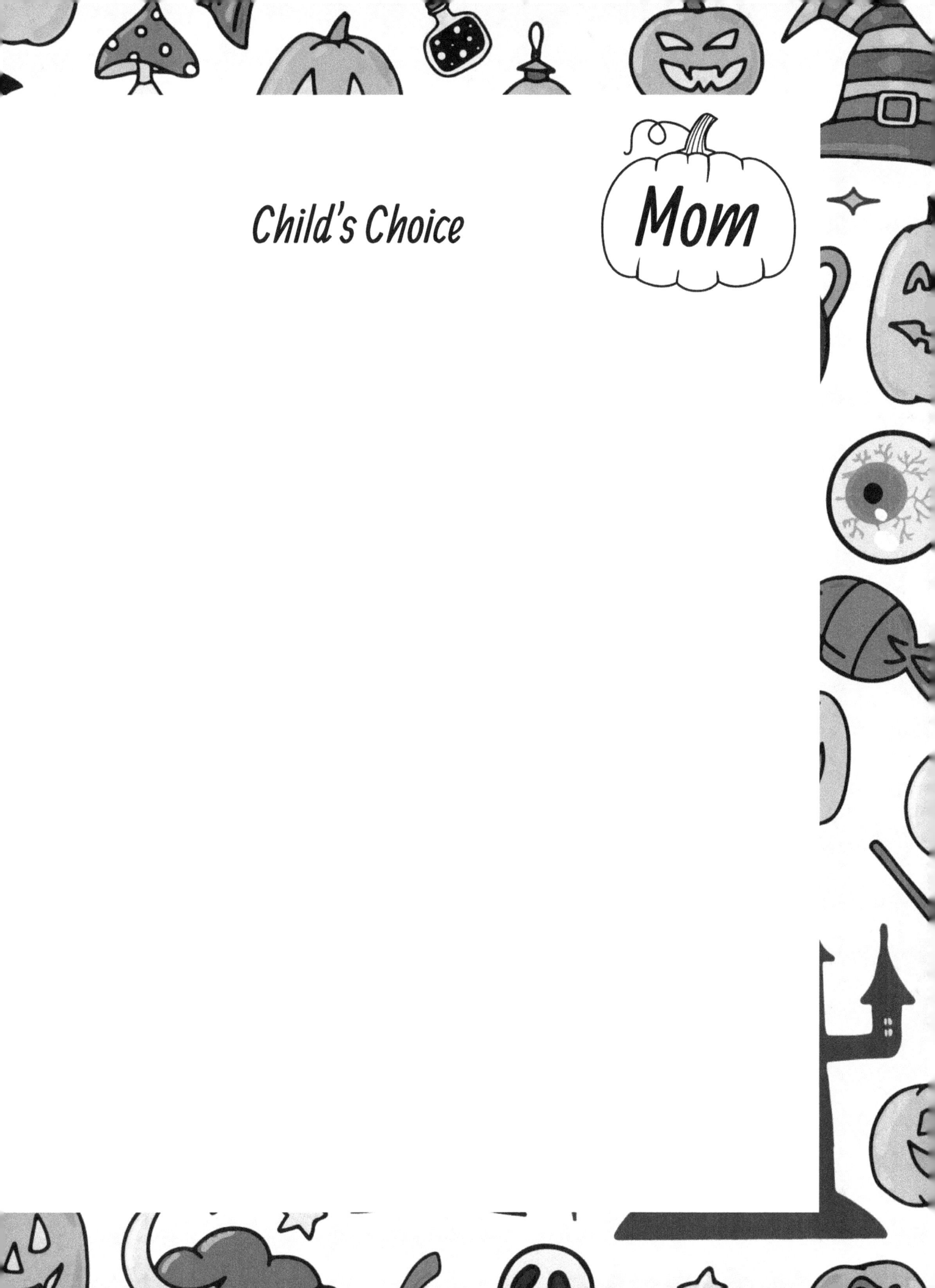

Mom

Child

Mom's Choice

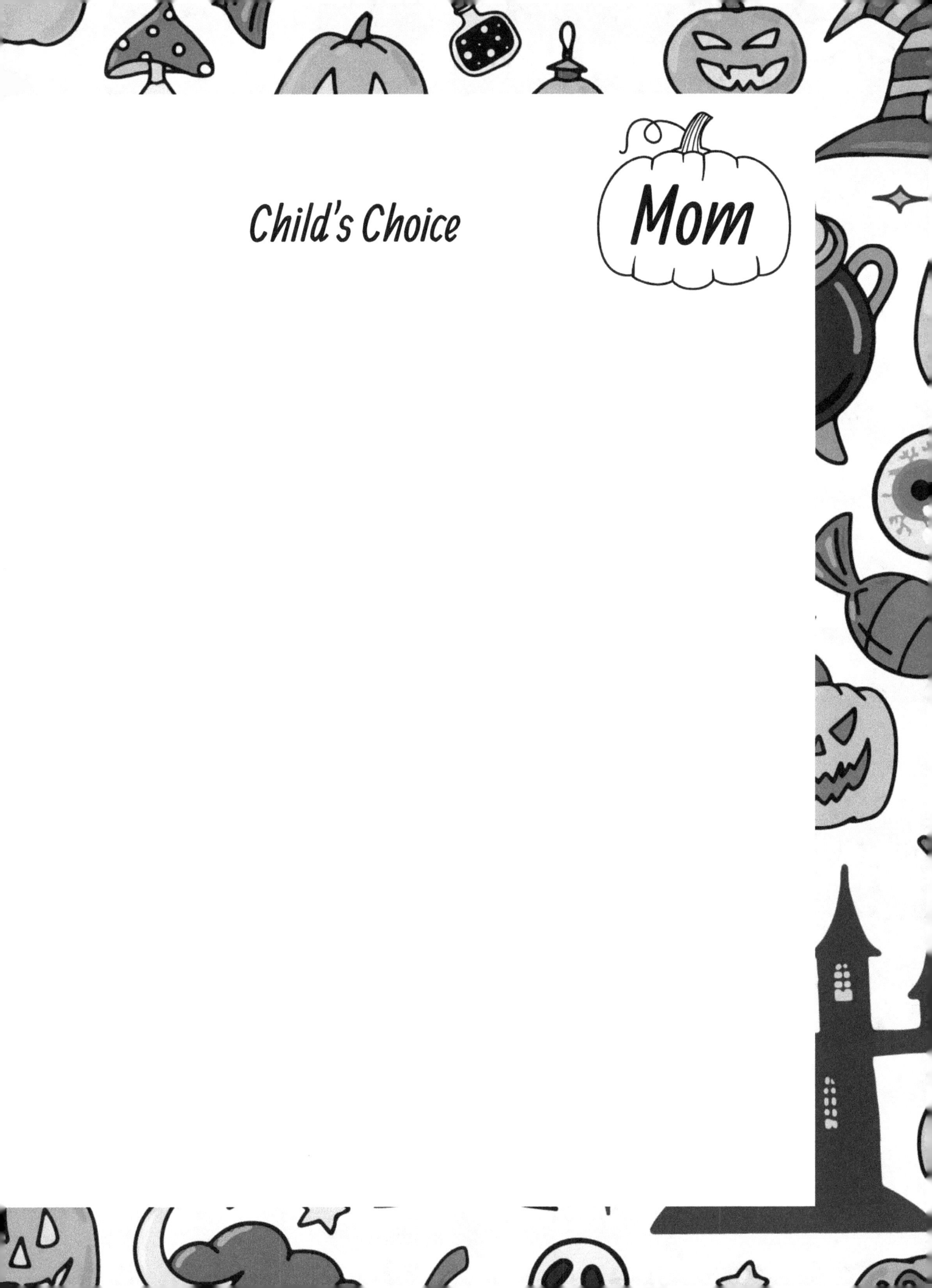

Child's Choice

Mom

Child

Mom's Choice

Child's Choice

Mom

Bonus
Coloring
Pages

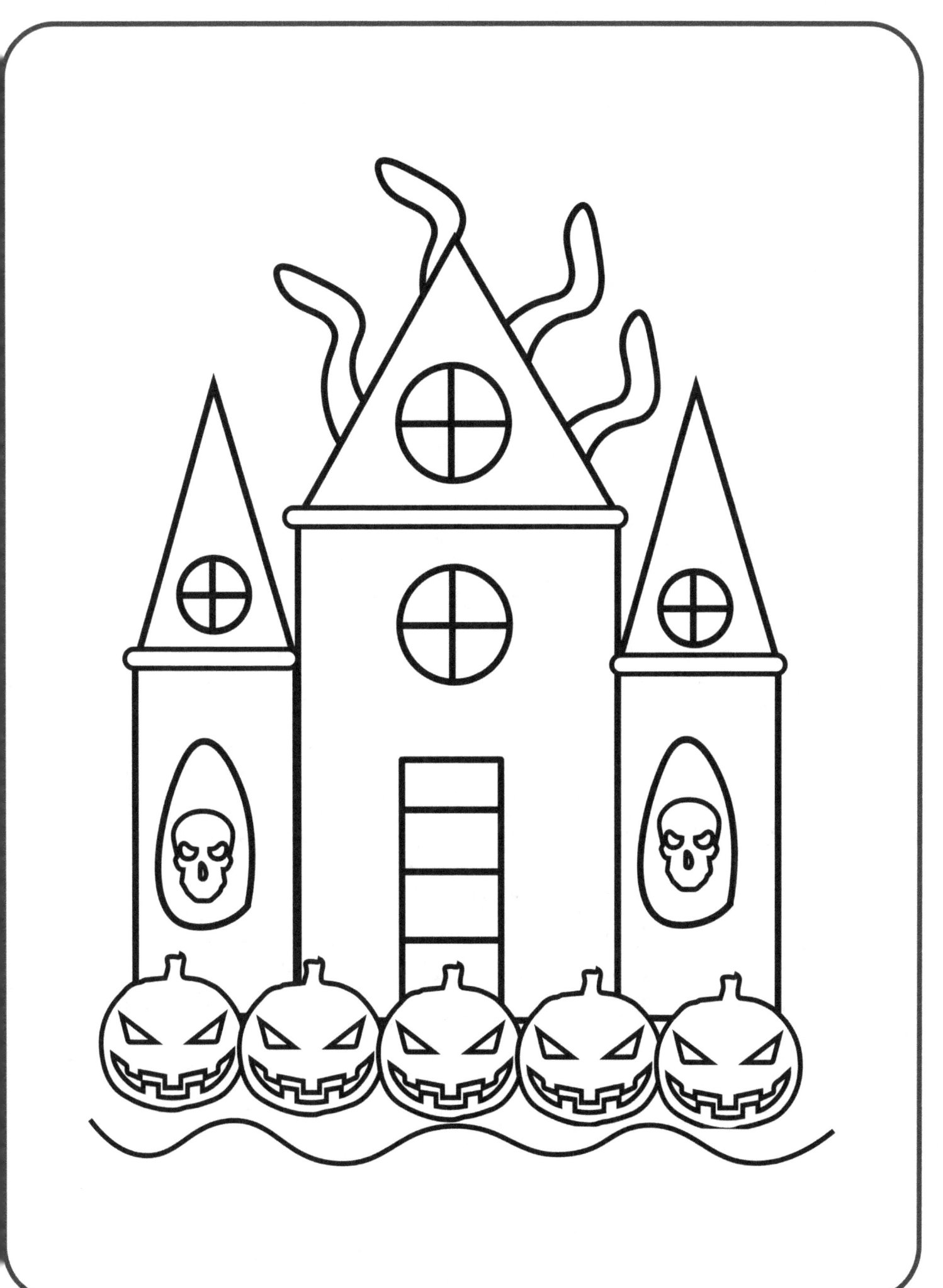

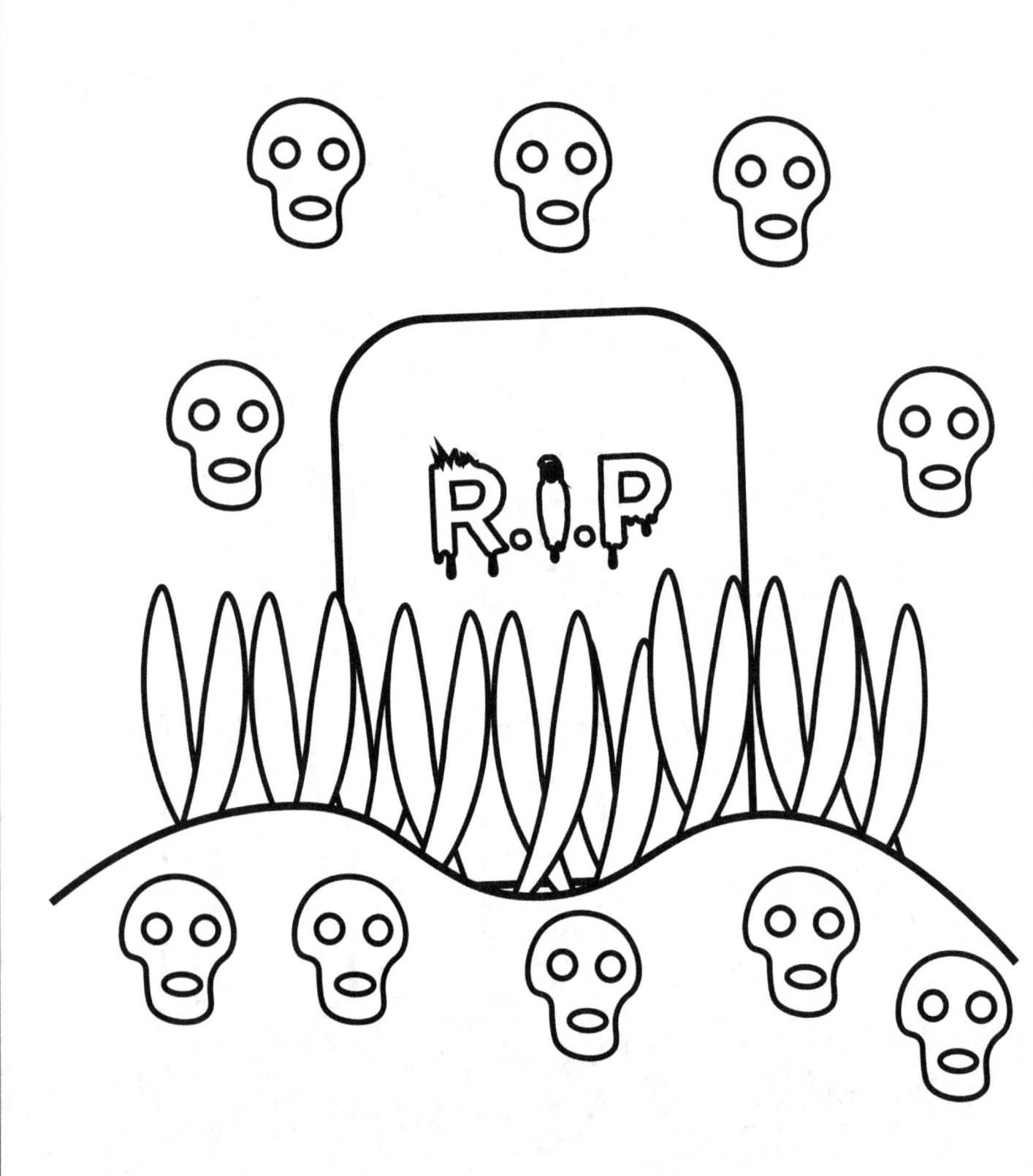

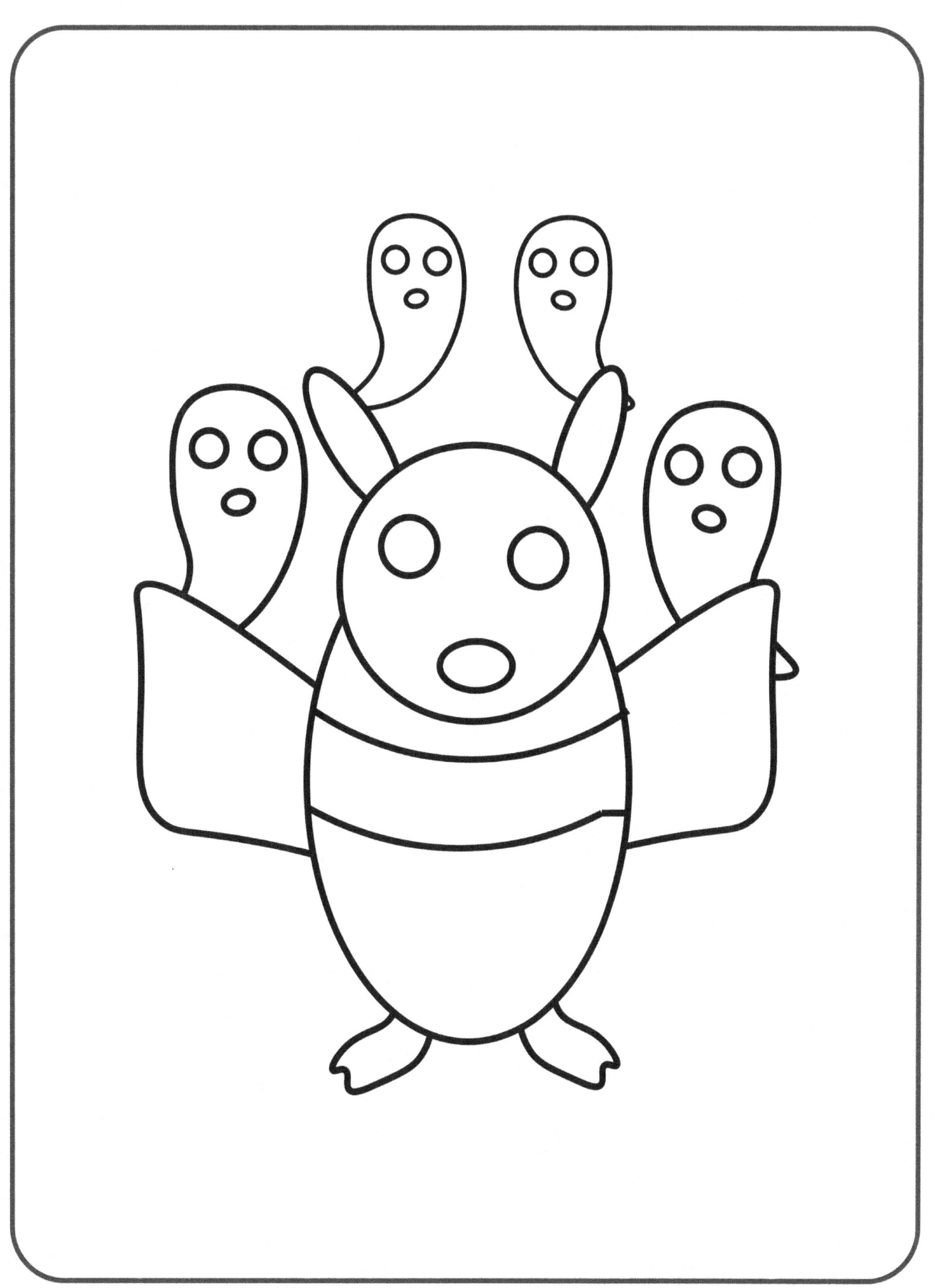

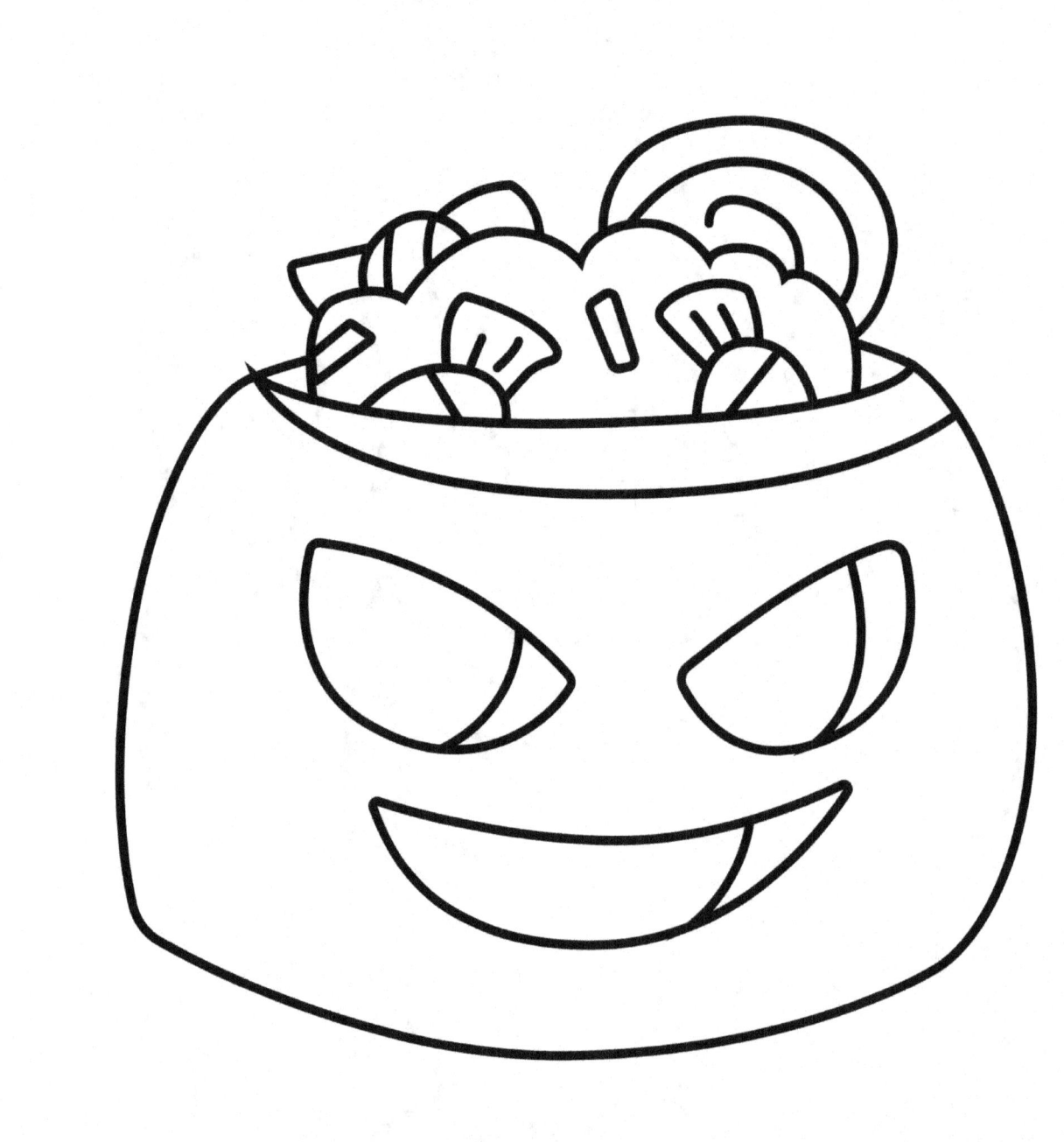

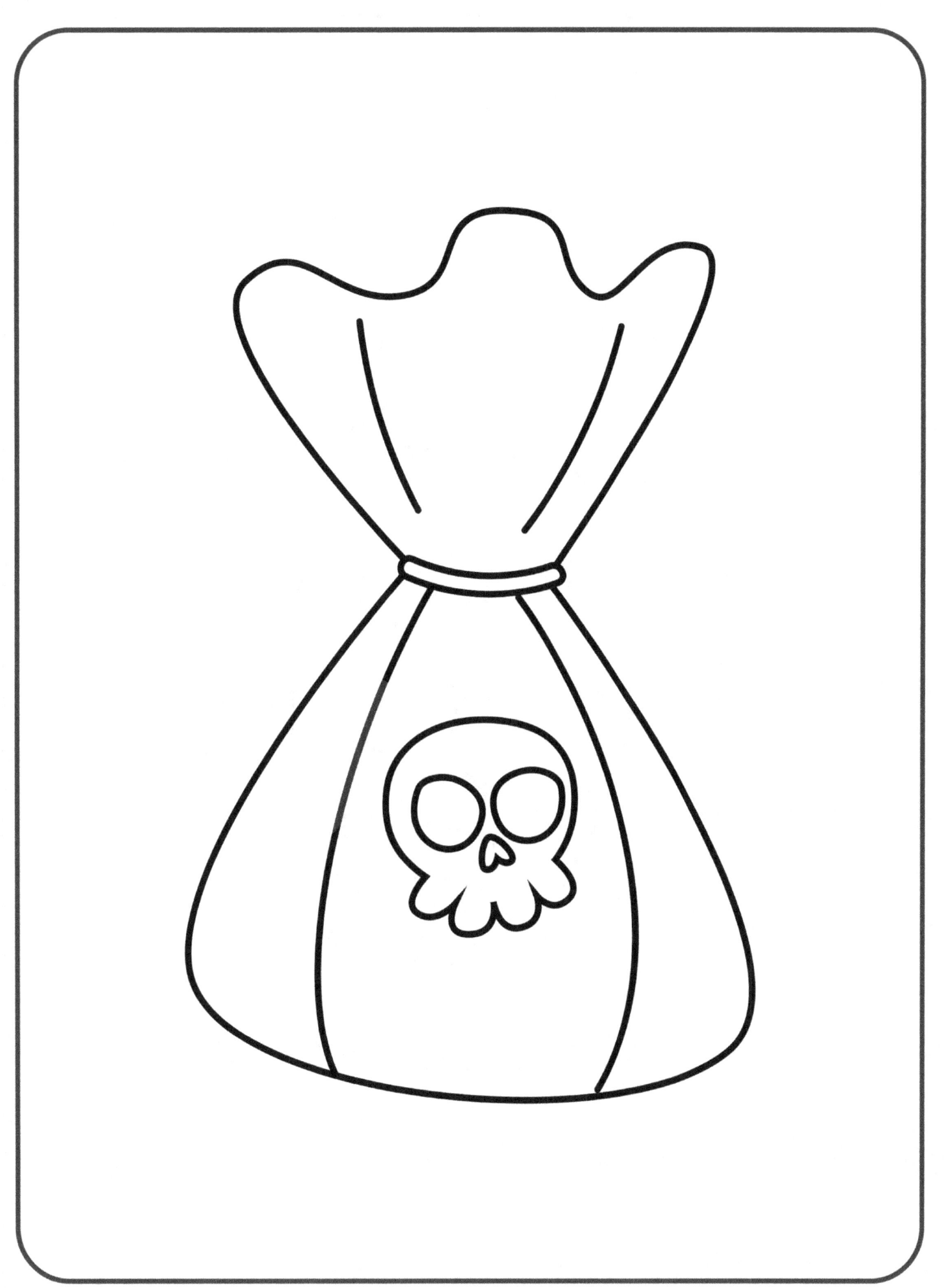

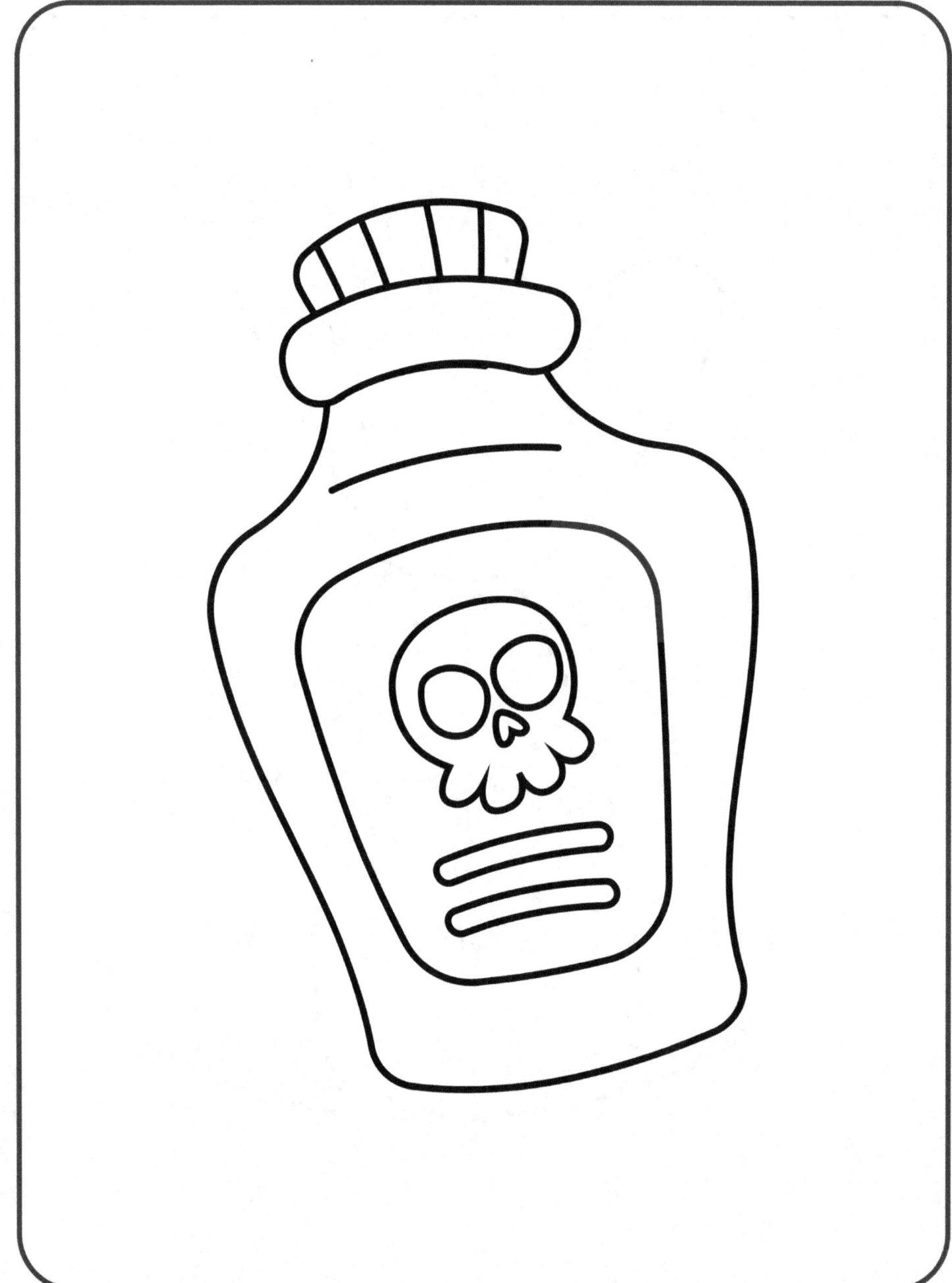

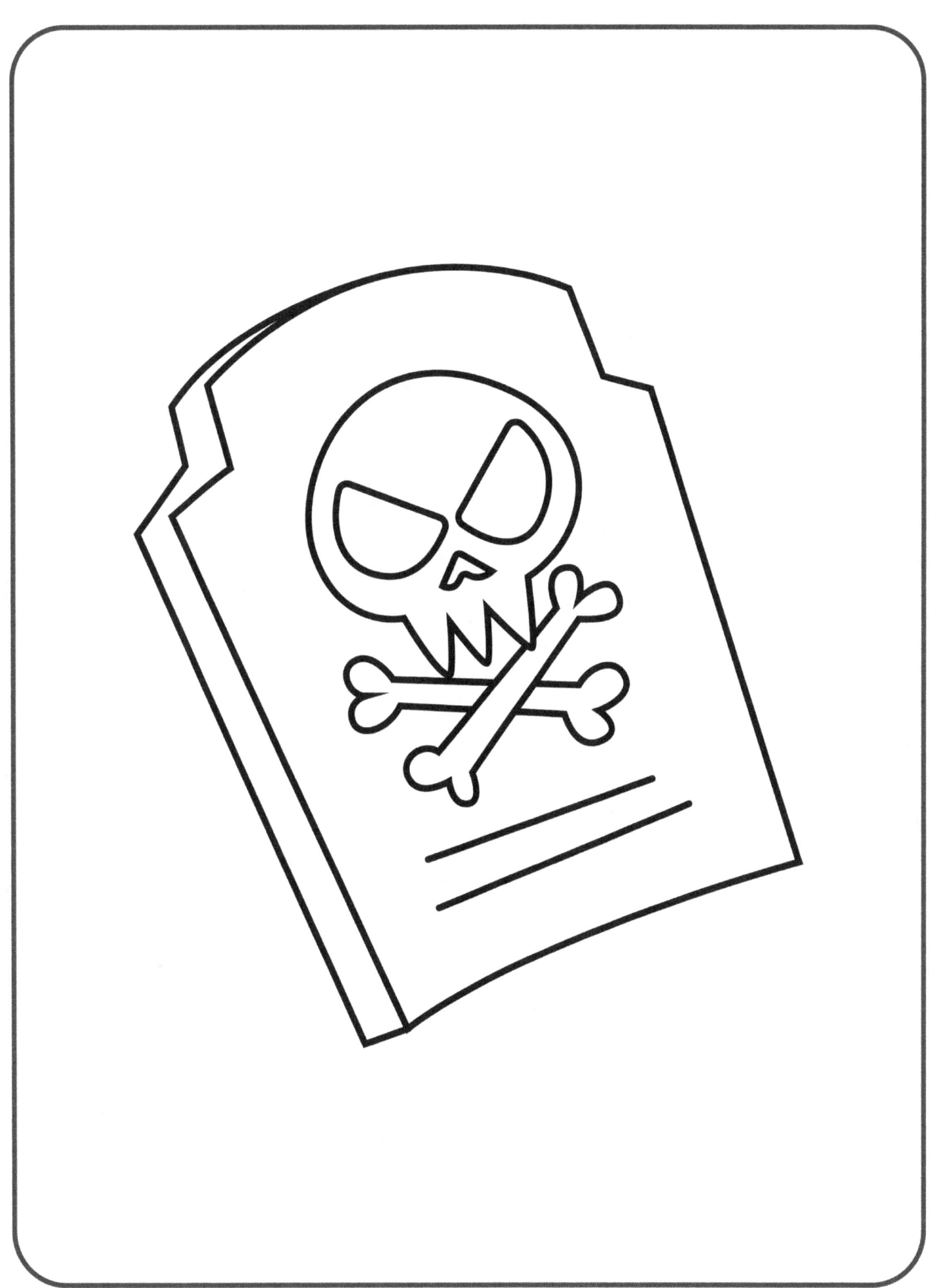

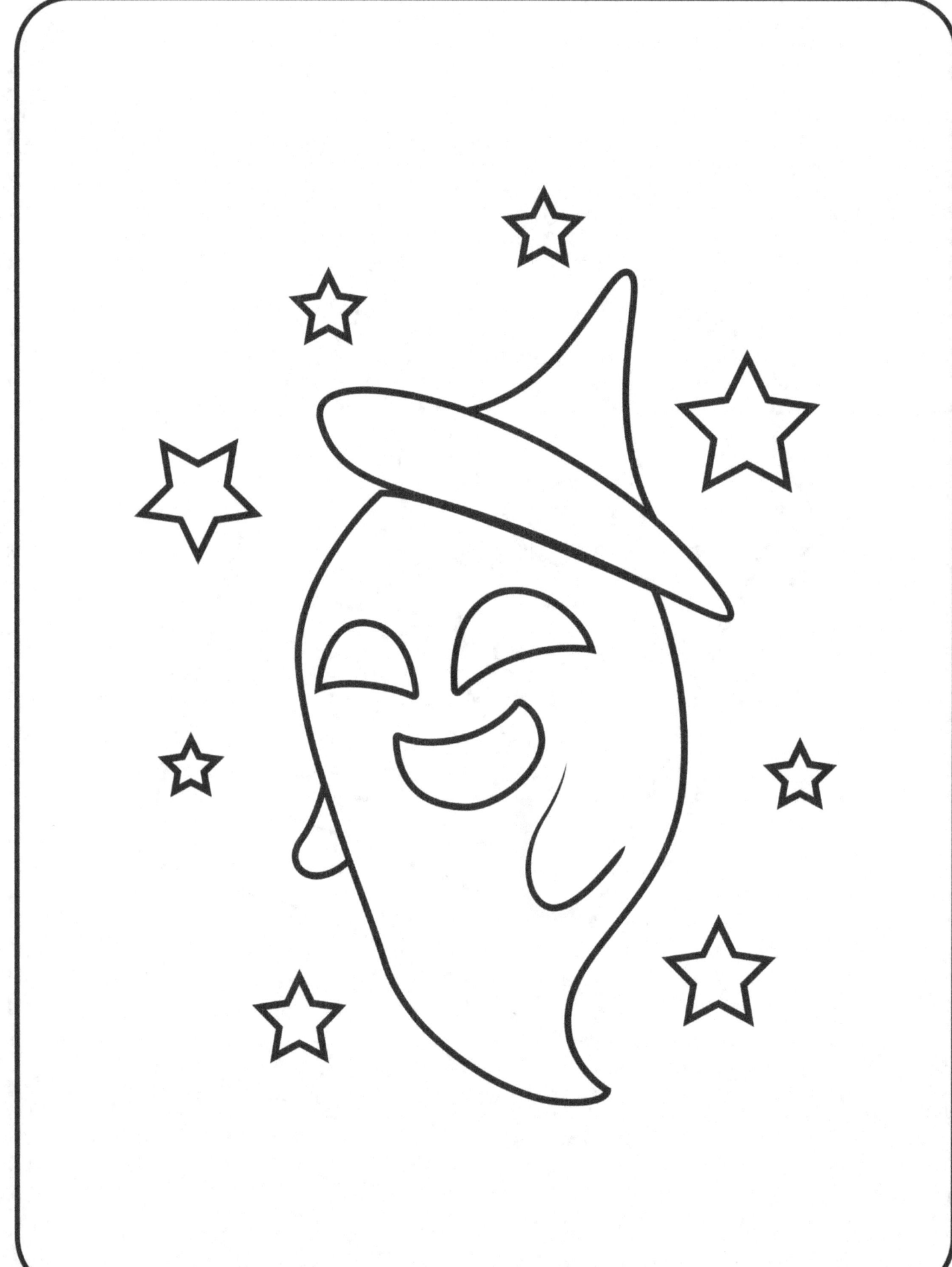

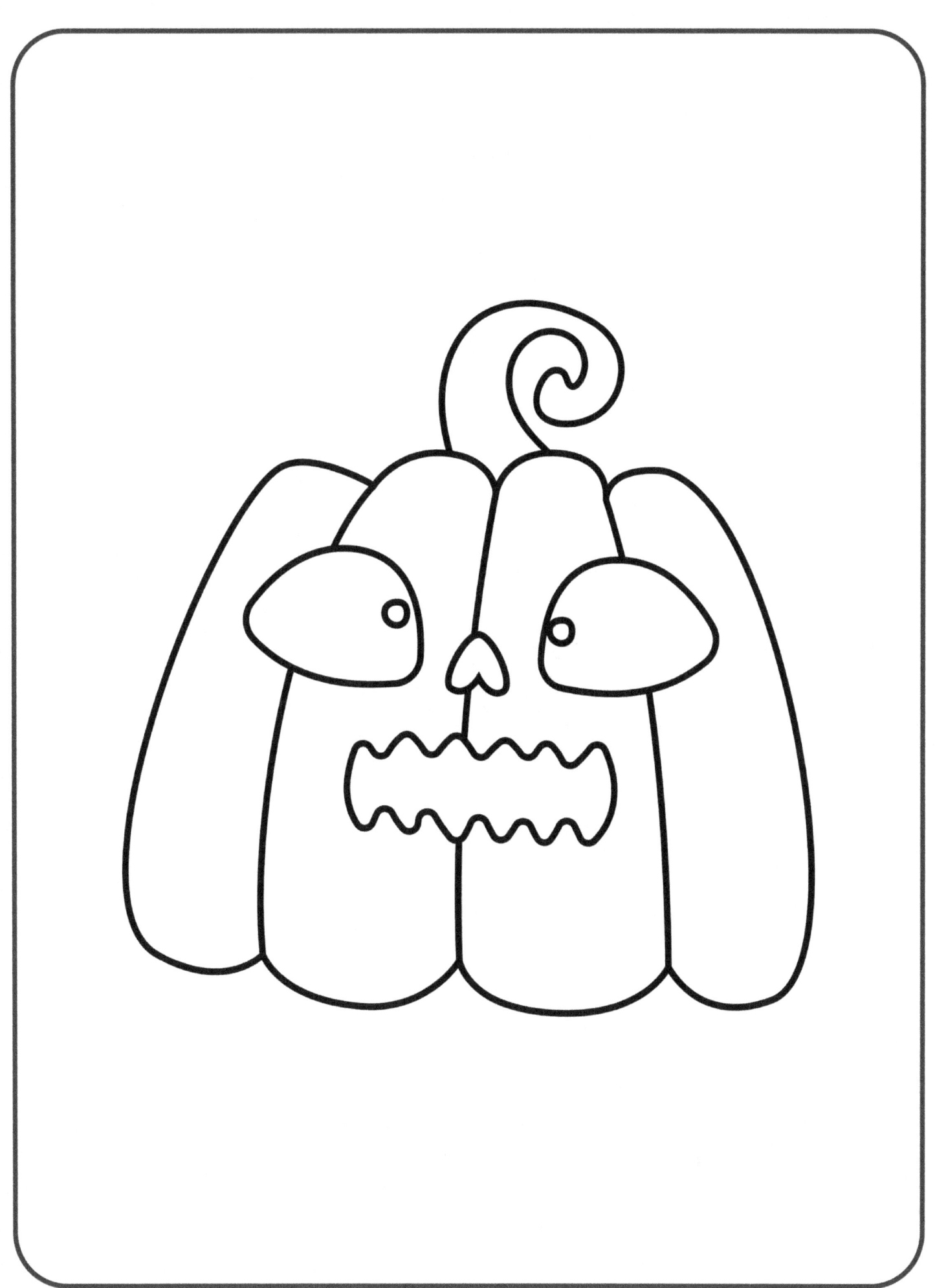

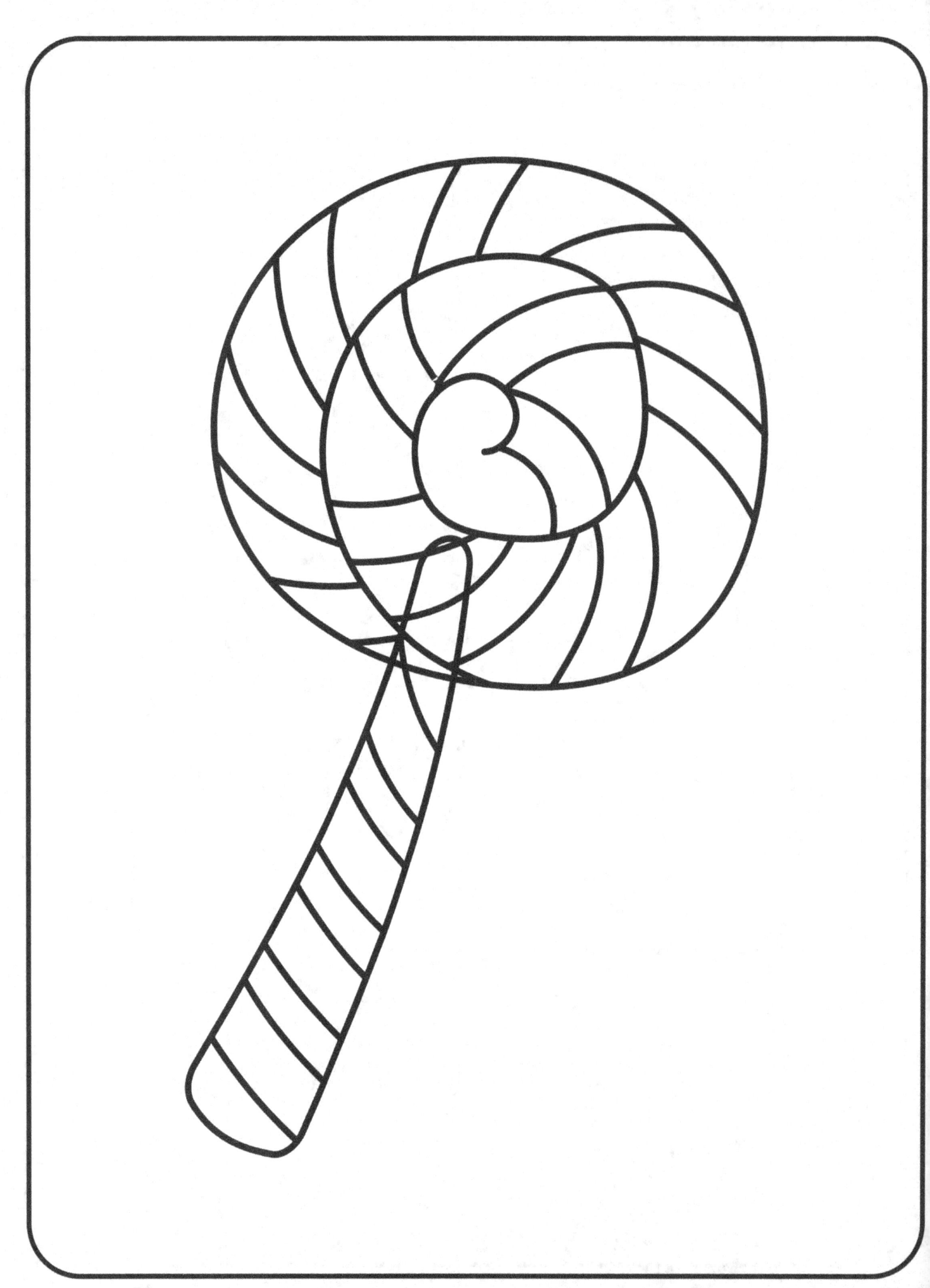